Evangelism & Politics

Evangelism & Politics

A Christian Perspective on the Church and the State

JOHN C. BARRETT

WIPF & STOCK · Eugene, Oregon

EVANGELISM & POLITICS
A Christian Perspective on the Church and the State

Wipf & Stock
An Imprint of Wipf and Stock Publishers
199 W. 8th Ave., Suite 3
Eugene, OR 97401

www.wipfandstock.com

www.professorbarrett.com

PAPERBACK ISBN: 978-1-7252-6374-1
HARDCOVER ISBN: 978-1-7252-6365-9
EBOOK ISBN: 978-1-7252-6366-6

Manufactured in the U.S.A. 02/10/20

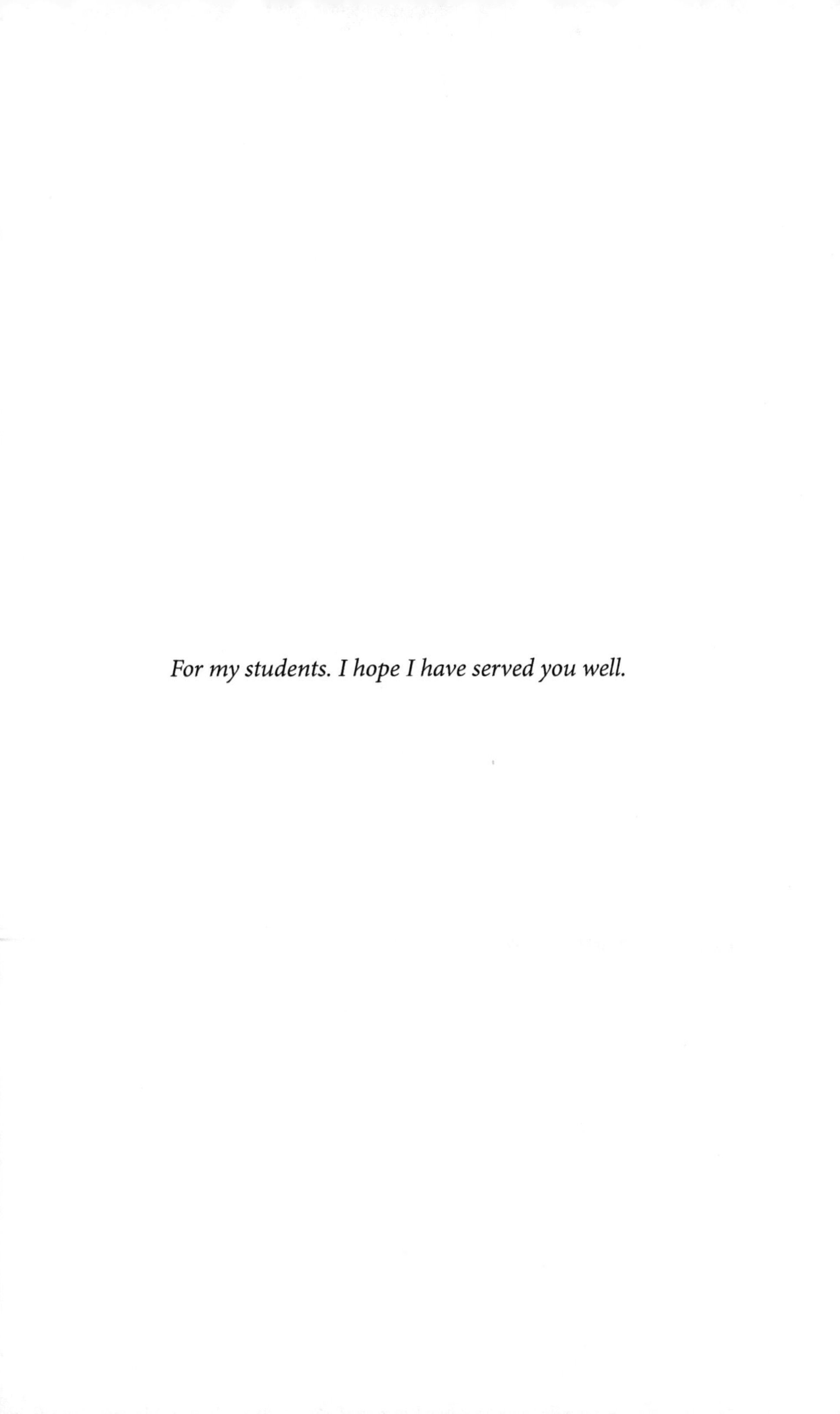

For my students. I hope I have served you well.

Contents

Acknowledgments

I would first like to thank my wife Karen for all her love, support, and encouragement. I owe her a great debt for all her efforts to care for our seven children: Nissah, Christian, William, Jonah, Annah, David, and Isaac. Her selfless labors allow me to study, teach, and spend time writing.

I would also like to thank Dallas Baptist University and especially LeTourneau University for giving me the wonderful opportunity to teach political science classes that integrate faith and learning. I doubt this book would exist were it not for these institutions allowing me to (at least try to) disciple students within the context of government and politics.

I would like to thank the many wonderful faculty members at Baylor University who taught me so much about religion, politics, and church-state relations. I also feel a debt to Reformed Theological Seminary. Although I have never enrolled there as a student, over the years I have listened to the countless audio lectures that they offer online—enough that I feel I know faculty members. By making these available to the public, RTS taught me much about theology.

Finally, I would like to thank my parents for their endless and overwhelming support in every endeavor I undertake. At every step in my life, they have provided love and encouragement.

Any wisdom you find in these pages came from God. Any fallacies you find in these pages came from me.

Introduction

This short work was a long time coming. For much of my life, I have been passionate about both discipleship and politics, but they always appeared to be two distinct roles. Some Christians were called to disciple through the church; others were called to govern through the state. I saw very little overlap between the two roles. My passion for discipleship pulled me away from political engagement. And yet I was still passionate about both.

In the early 2000s, I found myself trying to find some common ground between the two, searching for a career that would allow me to disciple and be involved in politics. I explored careers with various Christian organizations that were engaged in government affairs and then in 2006, on a whim, I began teaching political science classes at Dallas Baptist University as an adjunct professor. At last, I had found a sliver of overlap between discipleship and politics. The classes provided a venue for me to discuss the questions I was struggling to answer, a Bible study of sorts, on the relationship between Christians and their government. I would present questions and Scriptures. The students would respond with thoughts and discussion. At some point, they would ask what I thought to which I would just shrug. I was trying to work out answers myself.

That experience ultimately led to a PhD and a career change. My dissertation explored the political dynamics of mission work in the Middle East—what impact did US foreign policy have on evangelism and vice versa? In 2015, I became a full-time professor at LeTourneau University where the discussions between my students and me continued. Somewhere around 2018, mental light bulbs began to turn on. I saw a picture of discipleship through political engagement slowly emerge from my study of Scripture, political theology, and classroom discussions. Jotting down notes in fits and starts eventually led to writing paragraphs. By late 2019, I had completed an initial draft of this work.

When the dust settled, I saw politics not as a separate field from evangelism but as a field for evangelism—one that Christians should be engaged in. My hope in writing this book is that other, evangelically minded-Christians who are interested in politics will have an easier (if not to say quicker) time of seeing how their role in government and politics can serve as an evangelistic witness to society. At last, I have a few opinions to share with my students when they ask me, "Professor, what do you think?"

Part 1

Principles

GOD'S SOVEREIGNTY

A Christian perspective on government and politics should begin with God's sovereignty. Moreover, the role of God's sovereignty should not be marginal. God should not be viewed simply as the deistic creator of government and politics, nor as just a referee issuing rules for government and politics—this reduces the Christian faith to a mere code of ethics. From a Christian perspective, God should be seen as an active participant and, more than that, the primary actor in politics. God is in utter control of all things, and his control cannot be challenged let alone wrested from him. This is true not only of individual lives but also of the grand sweep of history including empires and kings. God is the author of history. "He controls the course of world events; he removes kings and sets up other kings."[1] In the Old Testament, the mighty kingdoms of Egypt, Israel, Assyria, Babylon, Persia, and Rome are puppets in his hands. God makes one kingdom rise and another fall. God places one person in authority and deposes another.

1. See Daniel 2:21.

In the book of Exodus, God hardens Pharaoh's heart and drowns the Egyptian army in order to establish the Israelites as an independent nation. In the book of Joshua and Judges, God inflicts defeat after defeat on Israel's enemies, no matter the military odds, so long as Israel remains faithful. In the book of 2 Samuel, God causes David to take a census of Israel in order to punish the nation for its unfaithfulness.[2] In the book of 2 Kings, God has the Assyrians and Babylonians conquer Israel as punishment for its unfaithfulness. In the book of Daniel, God humbles Nebuchadnezzar, overthrows Belshazzar, and predicts the rise and fall of Persia, Greece, and Rome. In the book of Matthew, Christ declares that he has "all authority on heaven and on earth."[3] In the book of Revelation, Christ defeats a numberless army with one swift action, on two occasions.[4]

God's sovereignty should not merely be a doctrine that is affirmed but rather a founding principle that has a very real impact on the way Christians politically think, speak, and act. Christians should draw peace, strength, and courage from the fact that no matter who gains political authority or what policies they enact, God's authority is still firmly and irrevocably in place, and God's purposes cannot be thwarted.

The Bible presents many examples where faith in God's sovereignty concretely influences the political actions of leaders. Moses boldly confronts Pharaoh because he knows God is sovereign. Joshua daringly attacks the formidable kingdoms in the Promised Land because he knows God is sovereign. David imprudently challenges Goliath because he knows God is sovereign. Jeremiah audaciously calls on Judah to surrender to the Babylonians because he knows God is sovereign. Daniel accepts the delay of Israel's restoration because he knows God is sovereign. Perhaps the best examples, however, are the two occasions when David spares Saul's life.

In 1 Samuel 24, David and his men are running for their lives, hiding at the back of a dark cave while Saul obsessively seeks to kill them. Saul unwittingly goes into the cave alone to relieve himself.

2. See 2 Samuel 24:1.

3. See Matthew 28:18.

4. See Revelation 19:21 and 20:9.

David's men interpret it as a God-given opportunity to kill Saul and gain the throne. "'Now's your opportunity!' David's men whispered to him. 'Today the LORD is telling you, "I will certainly put your enemy into your power, to do with as you wish."'"[5] In 1 Samuel 26, another opportunity arises when David sneaks into Saul's camp undetected because Saul's troops have all fallen asleep.

David has every reason to kill Saul. Saul had repeatedly tried to murder him in spite of his loyal and effective service. God moreover had already anointed David to be the king of Israel and rejected Saul for unfaithfulness.[6] David could have taken matters into his own hands and tried to carry out God's plan on his own time, but he refuses. "The LORD forbid that I should do this to my lord the king. I shouldn't attack the LORD's anointed one, for the LORD himself has chosen him."[7]

David's actions make no sense from a worldly perspective. In bewilderment, Saul himself declares, "Who else would let his enemy get away when he had him in his power?"[8] David's actions only make sense under the assumption that God is sovereign. David acts in the confidence that God's plan does not hinge on a sinful act of rebellion. David knows God will end Saul's life and reign when he sees fit. "'No!' David said. 'Don't kill him. For who can remain innocent after attacking the Lord's anointed one? Surely the Lord will strike Saul down someday, or he will die of old age or in battle.'"[9] So great is David's confidence in God's sovereignty, that even Saul acknowledges it. "And now I realize that you are surely going to be king, and that the kingdom of Israel will flourish under your rule."[10] In this way, David's political act of faith is an evangelistic witness to those around him.

God's sovereignty is a key principle for a Christian perspective on politics, and David provides a good example of how tangibly

5. See 1 Samuel 24:4.
6. See 1 Samuel 15.
7. See 1 Samuel 24:6.
8. See 1 Samuel 24:19.
9. See 1 Samuel 26:9–10.
10. See 1 Samuel 24:20.

trusting in God's sovereignty leads us to make political decisions that glorify him. God had decreed that David would be the king of Israel—his plan did not require rebellion on David's part to achieve it. God is not only completely sovereign but also completely trustworthy. God can be trusted with government and politics. Humanity, in contrast, is completely untrustworthy, which leads to a second key principle for a Christian perspective on politics.

HUMANITY'S SINFULNESS

Political theories assume that human nature is either inherently good or bad. Those assuming it is bad, see government restraining humanity's sinful impulses. Those assuming it is good, see government enabling humanity's goodness to shine forth. A Christian perspective on politics should assume that humanity is inherently bad—that is, our natural inclination is to evil and not good—to be selfish rather than selfless. The Bible makes this abundantly clear:

> The Lord looks down from heaven
> on the entire human race;
> he looks to see if anyone is truly wise,
> if anyone seeks God.
> But no, all have turned away;
> all have become corrupt.
> No one does good,
> not a single one![11]

Humanity is inherently sinful because of Adam's rebellion in the garden of Eden. "When Adam sinned, sin entered the world. Adam's sin brought death, so death spread to everyone, for everyone sinned."[12] Hardship, pain, sickness, and death would now be ever-present in the world. Moreover, our pure, intimate relationship with God was broken, depriving us of our deepest longing—the eternal, unconditional love we all need, by design. Humanity

11. See Psalm 14:2–3.

12. See Romans 5:12.

became enslaved to sin. Christians, thanks only to the supernatural power of the Holy Spirit, are able to resist sinful inclinations, but even they will repeatedly yield to temptation. As the apostle Paul himself wrote, "I know that nothing good lives in me, that is, in my sinful nature. I want to do what is right, but I can't. I want to do what is good, but I don't. I don't want to do what is wrong, but I do it anyway."[13] Humanity's sinful inclinations, moreover, will persist until Christ returns. No political, educational, or economic system can cure the world of the terminal disease of sin.

Like God's sovereignty, humanity's sinfulness should not merely be a doctrine that is affirmed but rather a founding principle that has a very real impact on the way Christians politically think, speak, and act. Christians should have limited confidence in any political leader no matter the leader's political or religious views. "Don't put your confidence in powerful people; there is no help for you there. When they breathe their last, they return to the earth, and all their plans die with them."[14] Political leaders almost invariably claim they can make the world better if they can just gain enough power. In democratic countries, election campaigns use such claims to whip supporters into a frenzied, false hope of political progress. Christians should not fall prey to these illusions and recognize that even the best of political leaders are but mere sinners.

This pessimistic view of human nature is part of the argument for limiting the powers of government and individual leaders. The founders of the United States established political rights and the system of checks and balances because they expected political leaders, no matter who they were, to misuse their power if it was unlimited and unchecked. The Constitutional system, therefore, restrains any political leader from gaining too much power by widely distributing power throughout the system. International power presents a similar problem.

All states use their power for selfish gain, to varying degrees, because of the sinfulness of humanity. It is not merely one nation that is corrupt but all nations. Yet the international system lacks

13. See Romans 7:18–19.

14. See Psalm 146:3–4.

the formal checks and balances that distribute power widely and prevent any one nation from becoming too dominant. The more power a nation gains, the more it will be tempted to misuse that power and to quote Lord Acton, "Power tends to corrupt and absolute power corrupts absolutely."

Political leaders are not the only ones with an inclination towards evil—ordinary citizens are sinners too. Christians should be skeptical about how citizens will respond to laws and government programs. People, as sinners, will inevitably seek to take advantage of the political system they are in by exploiting assistance programs (a temptation of the poor), tax codes (a temptation of the wealthy) or by outright breaking the law. Christians should not be surprised but rather expect this and advocate for policies that assume people will inevitably attempt to exploit and circumvent the law for their own advantage.

Likewise, Christians should recognize that citizens will act selfishly but not necessarily "rationally" or "responsibly." We are spiritual creatures, first and foremost. Our spiritual state greatly influences our emotional state, which greatly influences the choices we make. Our sinful nature turns us into fools. As Christ said, "Anyone who hears my teaching and doesn't obey it is foolish, like a person who builds a house on sand. When the rains and floods come and the winds beat against that house, it will collapse with a mighty crash."[15] All sins are "irrational" because they all take us away from Christ—the one person who can satisfy our deepest longing. On the contrary, all sin leads to death. If we were rational, we would not sin. But we are not rational, we are sinners and, for this reason, we sin, oftentimes to the point of death. "An evil man is held captive by his own sins; they are ropes that catch and hold him. He will die for lack of self-control; he will be lost because of his great foolishness."[16] Christians should therefore not expect citizens to always act "rationally" or "responsibly" and be leery of policies that rest on such erroneous assumptions.

15. See Matthew 7:26–27.

16. See Proverbs 5:22–23.

Perhaps most importantly, Christians should acknowledge the limits of political progress no matter how well policies are designed and executed. Life on earth will continue to be marked by hardship, pain, sickness, and death until Christ returns and rids the world of sin once and for all. Even the best of governments cannot change the fact that in a fallen world, our deepest longings for security, prosperity, and love cannot be fully realized. We were not designed to live in a sinful world. We were designed to be completely loved by a holy God while we immortally live in the luxurious paradise of his kingdom. Life on earth will inevitably be disappointing in comparison. Efforts to wring satisfaction out of the world around us will inevitably fail because satisfaction can only be found in Christ, and he is usually the last place we look for it. Yet as Paul wrote, "what we suffer now is nothing compared to the glory he will reveal to us later."[17]

The fallen state of man is a second foundational principle of a Christian perspective on politics. Christians should have limited expectations for political leaders, citizens, and governments in general. All will fall into temptation and selfishly but futilely seek satisfaction from a world that cannot provide it. Christ alone can cure the world of the disease of sin.

THE KINGDOM OF GOD VS. EARTHLY GOVERNMENT

Contrasting the kingdom of God with earthly governments sheds light on the relationship between the two. In part, we can think of the kingdom of God as heaven. It is an eternal, presently invisible, spiritual realm with political, economic, and social structures. In heaven, Christ rules completely and directly. The immortal citizens of heaven live in luxury and have no need for money or material gain. Moreover, its citizens are in perfect relationship with God—whom they worship—and each other. There is no conflict let alone hardship, pain, sickness, and death. In the kingdom of God, we find

17. See Romans 8:18.

complete fulfillment of our deepest longing—something earthly kingdoms can never provide.

At the same time, the kingdom of God, as an eternal, presently invisible, spiritual realm, overlaps with the current world. To use Jesus' words: "The Kingdom of God can't be detected by visible signs. You won't be able to say, 'Here it is!' or 'It's over there!' For the Kingdom of God is already among you."[18] The Holy Spirit is present in the current world and, in this sense, the kingdom of God is present here and now. Christians have the Holy Spirit living within them and are part of the kingdom of God—they are citizens who do not yet fully live within the kingdom. The kingdom of God, moreover, expands here on earth whenever the Holy Spirit enters someone thus making the person a citizen of heaven who, while on earth, will acknowledge their helpless, sinful state, accept the grace of Christ, and desire to submit to Christ's authority. To the extent that Christians live in accordance with God's will, they present an example to the world, a sweet foretaste, of what life will be like the kingdom of heaven.

Earthly governments, in contrast, are the temporary, visible, material, political, economic, and social structures we are all too familiar with. Earthly governments (try to) monopolize violence and establish a societal order. That order benefits society. If the benefits are dispersed across a wide spectrum of society, the order is relatively just. If the benefits are concentrated in a narrow spectrum of society, the order is relatively unjust.

In any event, earthly governments come and go as do political leaders. They cannot fully satisfy our deepest longings. At their best, earthly governments broadly provide a limited measure of security and prosperity to grateful citizens, who understand that earthly governments are incapable of providing anything more. That is to say, earthly governments can marginally mitigate the hardship, pain, sickness, and death we experience in life by partially restraining the sinful impulses of humanity and providing a few meager necessities. This is earthly government at its best. At its worst, earthly government encourages the unrestrained, lustful

18. See Luke 17:20–21.

pursuit of wealth, power, and pleasure on the part of the rulers and their supporters—material ends that even if obtained cannot fulfill our deepest longing. The difference may seem enormous from an earthly perspective but from an eternal perspective, the difference lasts but a few fleeting moments and is then forgotten.

The kingdom of God and earthly governments thus have very different perspectives of the world. Christ's coming and the gospel message was the joyous inauguration of the kingdom of God and the culmination of human history to that point. At the start of his public ministry, Christ declared, "The time of the LORD's favor has come."[19] Likewise, Christ's death on the cross was an earth-shattering event that irrevocably changed the world and God's relationship with it. Yet from the perspective of earthly governments, the early death of a wandering, homeless, teacher whose disciples abandoned and betrayed him was an insignificant event.

Similarly, earthly governments have a very different perspective on the gospel. Earthly governments can make use of "religions" with a spiritual economy, that is, a system whereby eternal rewards or punishments are offered in exchange for good or bad works here on earth. These systems conveniently keep citizens in line—provided that the "good works" don't run contrary to the interests of the state. The gospel, however, is problematic because it unconditionally offers God's grace to the vilest of sinners. No "good works" are necessary, just a humble, penitent heart. Nothing but the Holy Spirit stands in the way of Christians taking their "get out of jail free card" and running amok. For this reason, earthly governments are more comfortable with religions that strictly enforce a moral code that is compatible with their laws—even if the "religion" in question is masquerading as Christianity.

Another sharp contrast is how wealth and power are viewed. Earthly governments see wealth and power as unequivocally good, and they make enormous efforts to increase their measure of both. They consider life's struggles, conversely, as unequivocally bad—problems to be solved through policy or ignored in the quest for wealth and power.

19. See Luke 4:19.

From the perspective of the kingdom of God, much of this earthly perspective is turned upside down. The Bible acknowledges that wealth can be a blessing from God.[20] Yet it also acknowledges the dangers of wealth. To quote Jesus, "I tell you the truth, it is very hard for a rich person to enter the Kingdom of Heaven. I'll say it again—it is easier for a camel to go through the eye of a needle than for a rich person to enter the Kingdom of God!"[21] Wealth is not inherently bad, but it presents temptations. Wealth can be a distraction, sapping our energy and attention away from the kingdom of God. This is why Christians are told to "Seek the Kingdom of God above all else," and warned, "Don't wear yourself out trying to get rich. Be wise enough to know when to quit."[22] Wealth tempts us to put trust our money rather than God.[23]

Likewise, trials and temptations, from the perspective of the kingdom of God, are not problems to be solved but tools through which God refines us. As Jesus' brother, James wrote:

> Dear brothers and sisters, when troubles of any kind come your way, consider it an opportunity for great joy. For you know that when your faith is tested, your endurance has a chance to grow. So let it grow, for when your endurance is fully developed, you will be perfect and complete, needing nothing.[24]

Trials and temptations foster spiritual growth by pushing us to trust God with problems we cannot solve on our own. They strip away

20. For example, Proverbs 10:22, "The blessing of the Lord makes a person rich, and he adds no sorrow with it." Likewise, Proverbs 22:4, "True humility and fear of the Lord lead to riches, honor, and long life."

21. See Matthew 19:23–24.

22. See Matthew 6:33 and Proverbs 23:4. For more on this, see Christ's commentary on wealth in Matthew 6:19 and the Parable of the Sower in Luke 8:14 where Christ warns that some hear the gospel but never grow into maturity because they are focused on wealth and comfort.

23. See Proverbs 11:4 where the Bible warns "Riches won't help on the day of judgment, but right living can save you from death." or Proverbs 18:11 "The rich think of their wealth as a strong defense; they imagine it to be a high wall of safety."

24. See James 1:2–4.

the illusion of independence and self-reliance. Security and prosperity, on the other hand, rarely encourage spiritual growth because they lead us to believe we are in control and have overcome the problems we face through our own power.[25]

All this is to say that earthly governments futilely focus on manipulating humanity's frustrating, material, and ephemeral, present while the kingdom of God focuses on humanity's fulfilling, spiritual, eternity. Earthly governments look at humanity's sinfulness and falsely perceive a dark, Darwinian world where only the strong, briefly survive by ruthlessly wielding power. They frantically seek wealth and power and see life's inherent challenges as problems to be solved. The kingdom of God looks at humanity's sinfulness and rejoices at the freedom from sin God's grace provides as well as the knowledge that soon the dark dross of this world will be stripped away to reveal the eternal paradise of heaven. Life's inherent challenges are how God refines the citizens of the kingdom of God. Wealth and power can be blessings so long as they do not consume our attention, energy, and trust. The two kingdoms have starkly different values and perspectives on the world.

THE CHURCH

The church consists of all the Christians in the world—that is to say, all those who have the Holy Spirit living within them. Of course, not all those with the Holy Spirit living within them openly meet together with other Christians to worship, minister, and disciple, and many people who do so do not have the Holy Spirit living within them. Worldly concerns motivate the actions of the latter group, not a love for Christ. The church is thus an invisible society whose presence, nevertheless, can be observed in very real ways—its members, citizens of the kingdom of God, are currently living, as "temporary residents and foreigners," within earthly kingdoms.[26]

The mission of the church is the Great Commission:

25. See the parable of the rich fool in Luke 12:13–21 for Jesus' teaching on this.

26. See 1 Peter 2:11.

> Jesus came and told his disciples, "I have been given all authority in heaven and on earth. Therefore, go and make disciples of all the nations, baptizing them in the name of the Father and the Son and the Holy Spirit. Teach these new disciples to obey all the commands I have given you. And be sure of this: I am with you always, even to the end of the age."[27]

The Great Commission is not only the mission of the church corporately but also the mission of every Christian individually regardless of their role in society. All Christians, no matter whether they are a preacher or pilot, a missionary or mother, an elder or welder, all have an equal share in and responsibility to fulfill the Great Commission. The work of the church is not carried out by a select number of "professional" Christians who are merely supported by the rest of the church.

The Great Commission is not a political or social project. Jesus did not command the church to go forth and make disciples because he wanted the church to reform government, politics, or society. Such goals are laughable because they grossly minimize the magnitude of humanity's fallen state. A political or social movement cannot redress the consequences of original sin. The church carries out its work so that it can participate in the expansion of God's kingdom. Only God himself can establish the fullness of his kingdom.[28]

At the same time, the work of the church will inevitably have political and social consequences. Governments, regardless of whether they are democracies or dictatorships, reflect societal values and behaviors. As the number and maturity of disciples increases, society and politics will change too. Yet we must not have false hopes in the political consequences of discipleship. Sin will persist on earth until Christ returns. Moreover, we must not confuse the side effect and the goal. The goal of the church is to make disciples not to change society and politics.

27. See Matthew 28:18–20.

28. If God and God alone knows when his kingdom will fully come, mere humans cannot be driving the process.

The church corporately fulfills the Great Commission in a number of ways. For one, the church, not government or society, articulates the standard of morality that all people are held accountable to. I say "articulates" because the church does not define morality so much as it communicates God's definition of morality to the world and, according to that standard—the only one that matters—all humanity falls hopelessly short save Christ alone. It is not enough to have "good" deeds or to refrain from the "worst" sins. As Christ warned, "Unless your righteousness is better than the righteousness of the teachers of religious law and the Pharisees, you will never enter the Kingdom of Heaven!"[29] But Christ, with his supreme act of self-sacrifice on the cross, transfers through the Holy Spirit his sinless righteousness onto Christians, mere sinners, so that we can become citizens of the kingdom of God. Thanks be to God! The church articulates God's standard of morality to the world in hopes that the world will humbly recognize that it falls short and turn to Christ for forgiveness. Societal norms and legal codes, in contrast, do not define morality—they merely outline a few guidelines that help society to function, at a basic level, in spite of its own sinfulness.

At times society as a whole grievously and collectively sins. When the church fails to recognize such sins, the consequences are devastating. When the church does recognize such sins, it should not judge non-Christians but rather corporately and individually acknowledge how Christians themselves have fallen short. Multiple Biblical examples illustrate this idea. In the book of Nehemiah, Nehemiah is told the grievous news that the returning exiles are in great trouble and disgrace. Rather than condemning gentiles, Nehemiah weeps, prays, fasts, and corporately confesses the sins of God's people. "I confess that we have sinned against you. Yes, even my own family and I have sinned! We have sinned terribly by not obeying the commands, decrees, and regulations that you gave us through your servant Moses."[30]

29. See Matthew 5:20.

30. See Nehemiah 1:6–7.

Likewise, when Daniel is grieving the destruction of Jerusalem, he prays, fasts, and corporately confesses the sins of God's people. "But we have sinned and done wrong. We have rebelled against you and scorned your commands and regulations. We have refused to listen to your servants the prophets, who spoke on your authority to our kings and princes and ancestors and to all the people of the land."[31] Notably, when Nehemiah and Daniel are confessing, they both use the term "we." They do not deny their own sinfulness but rather corporately confess the sins of God's people as a whole. Corporately confessing sin is an evangelistic witness that fulfills the Great Commission by acknowledging the church's own sinfulness in comparison to God's standard of morality.

Another way the church fulfills the Great Commission is by being holy, that is, by living in a manner distinct from non-Christians. "But now you must be holy in everything you do, just as God who chose you is holy. For the Scriptures say, 'You must be holy because I am holy.'"[32] Christians should be distinguished not so much by what they do but how they do it. Christians are called into a broad range of roles, none of which is inherently "Christian." Even the roles traditionally considered to be "Christian" such as preachers, pastors, missionaries, etc. are not exclusively played by Christians. Most religions have clergy of some kind and, in any event, non-Christians also play the role of the Christian preacher, pastor, missionary, etc. out of "selfish ambition."[33] Money, authority, and notoriety, even in limited quantities, can be enough to motivate non-Christians into these fields.

All roles present, to varying degrees, trials and temptations. The businessman will be tempted to short-change legal and contractual obligations; mothers will be tempted to say hurtful things to their children in a moment of frustration; pastors will be tempted to increase attendance and contributions by preaching what people want to hear and building luxurious churches. In any case, the trials

31. See Daniel 9:5–6.

32. See 1 Peter 1:15–16 where Peter cites Leviticus 11:44–45. For other examples see, Leviticus 19:2 or 20:7.

33. See Philippians 1:17.

and temptations inherent to each role create a tension between the role and holy living.

The world measures success by the extent to which the goals inherent to each role have been achieved. The business executive is judged by revenues and profits. The teacher is judged by how much the students learn. The mother is judged by how well her children behave. Even the pastor is judged by attendance and contributions. All of these goals will best be achieved when nothing else matters to the one pursuing them. For example, the businessman will best achieve revenues and profits if everything else (family, friends, employees, etc.) is secondary. The same is also true for the pastor, mother, or elected official.

On the other hand, those simultaneously pursuing two (or more) goals will be hindered by the inherent tension between them. The businessman seeking to simultaneously increase profits and employee satisfaction may find some common ground between the two, but inevitably there will be a tension that forces a choice or a compromise that diminishes the achievement of one or the other. All this is to say, the Christian is called to fulfill the Great Commission above all else, and single-minded pursuit of the Great Commission will inevitably diminish the Christian's effectiveness in achieving other goals—however noble they may be. As Christ said, "No one can serve two masters."[34] This is true even for those playing "Christian" roles in society. The non-Christian pastor who is not inhibited by concerns of the Great Commission will have an advantage over the Christian pastor who lovingly wields the "rod and the staff" in an effort to shepherd the congregation closer to God.

Christians thus should be distinguished not by the roles they play or how effective they are in those roles but how they play their roles. In short, the fruit of the spirit should mark the way Christians play their role: love, joy, peace, patience, kindness, goodness, faithfulness, gentleness, and self-control.[35] Of these, the fruit of love can particularly distinguish Christians, but we must differentiate between "selfish" love and "selfless" love.

34. See Matthew 6:24.

35. See Galatians 5:22–23.

Acts of "selfless" love are different from ordinary acts of "love." Ordinary acts of love occur when we have something to gain or little to lose. For example, if we give money to a church that in return provides certain benefits—activities for us and our children—such a transaction is hardly selfless and not unlike a variety of other clubs and organizations in society. Likewise, giving gifts to those who will give us gifts in return or inviting someone to dinner who will return the favor is not selfless.[36] Jesus drew this distinction in the Sermon on the Mount. "If you love only those who love you, what reward is there for that? Even corrupt tax collectors do that much. If you are kind only to your friends, how are you different from anyone else? Even pagans do that."[37]

Selfless love occurs when you love someone who cannot or will not love you back. Selfless love entails sacrifice. Christians are called to give money to the poor even though they cannot repay us.[38] Christians are called to love their enemies even though they persecute us.[39] Christians are called to give not just out of their abundance but sacrificially out of their poverty as well.[40] This kind of love truly distinguishes Christians and provides an evangelistic witness to society.

Although selfless love is an evangelistic witness, it is not a means to an end but an end in itself. Christians are called to love, not because good may result, but because the act itself is good and mirrors how Christ loves us. Christ does not love us because we can offer something in return—we have nothing to offer but our own sinfulness. In the same way, acts of selfless love may occasionally yield worldly benefits, but it is foolish to assume they will. This is the false picture painted by popular culture. The hero refuses to do wrong but somehow prevails nevertheless. This is also the

36. See Luke 14:12 where Christ comments on this example: "Then he turned to his host. 'When you put on a luncheon or a banquet,' he said, 'don't invite your friends, brothers, relatives, and rich neighbors. For they will invite you back, and that will be your only reward.'"

37. See Matthew 5:46–47.

38. See Luke 12:33.

39. See Matthew 5:44.

40. See Mark 12:41–44.

fundamental problem with many modern pacifists. They see non-violence merely as another means to an end rather than an end in itself. Acts of selfless love may be done in the hope that some benefit will result, but they are never done solely for that reason. Selfless love will be done even when it is apparent there will be no immediate benefit.

In the context of political power, selfless love can be seen in two ways. One is when power is used not just for the benefit of the authority wielding the power, but when it is used for the benefit of those who cannot or will not benefit the authority in return. For example, when power is used to help widows and orphans—those who in ancient Jewish society had little to offer in return—it stands in sharp contrast to how political power is typically used. Any ruler will use power to benefit themselves, their political supporters, or even more broadly, the state they govern which, after all, will only add to their personal power and prestige. Power may even be used in an attempt to court political favor from those who do not currently support the ruler but may be convinced to do so. The truly selfless use of power, conversely, will benefit those who have nothing to offer in return.

A second way selfless love can be seen in the use of power is when it is voluntarily restrained for no other reason than as an act of grace. David provides a good model. After his son Absalom rebels, David and his officials flee the capitol. Shimei, a disgruntled member of Saul's tribe, follows along hurling curses, dirt, and stones at them. David's general Abishai has had enough. "'Why should this dead dog curse my lord the king?'" Abishai son of Zeruiah demanded. Let me go over and cut off his head!'"[41] David, however, restrains Abishai simply as an act of faith and grace. "Leave him alone and let him curse, for the Lord has told him to do it. And perhaps the Lord will see that I am being wronged and will bless me because of these curses today."[42]

Selflessly restraining power provides an evangelistic witness because it stands in sharp contrast to how and why power is restrained

41. See 2 Samuel 16:9.

42. See 2 Samuel 16:11–12.

from a worldly perspective. Selfishly, power is sometimes restrained as a strategy for achieving an end. A nation, for example, may not use military force in order to win support from allies or to curry favor in the court of world opinion—both of which may ultimately achieve the end more effectively than raw use of military might. The truly selfless restraint of power, conversely, will be done even when there is nothing to gain in return—only something to lose. It is not merely a strategy for achieving ends through non-violent means.

Selfless love by definition entails risk. Sacrificially giving money to the poor leaves less money in reserve for emergencies. Sharing the gospel invites persecution and ridicule. Loving those who have hurt you opens the door to further injury. The parable of the Good Samaritan provides an illustrative example. The Samaritan takes a significant risk when he stops to help an injured man on a dangerous stretch of road. In our own modern context, it was akin to helping someone in an alley, in the bad part of town, at night.

The risks of selfless love are not just born by the individual but also, at times, by those under their authority. A father's generosity towards a ministry leaves less money for the whole family. An entire business may struggle because a business owner refuses to pay bribes or shows grace to a struggling employee. Christ's story of the lost sheep illustrates the risks of selfless love. "If a man has a hundred sheep and one of them gets lost, what will he do? Won't he leave the ninety-nine others in the wilderness and go to search for the one that is lost until he finds it?"[43] The shepherd puts the ninety-nine at risk when he leaves them to search for the one. In the same way, selfless love does not just put ourselves at risk but others as well. Nevertheless, Christians are called to selflessly love because it not only provides a witness to society, it deepens our faith by pushing us to rely on God as our protector—even if God's protection does not come in an immediate, worldly form. To quote Jesus, "Don't be afraid of those who want to kill your body; they cannot touch your soul. Fear only God, who can destroy both soul and body in hell."[44]

43. See Luke 15:4.

44. See Matthew 10:28.

Christians are often discouraged from selflessly loving (by other Christians no less) when selfless love is presented as the false choice of imagined extremes rather than the practical realities we usually find ourselves in. For example, someone will argue against generosity, saying, "You cannot give away all your money, because you must take care of your own family." In reality, the dilemma the person actually faces is whether to give $100 to a ministry or take their family out for dinner one more time. Likewise, if someone is struggling to respond non-violently to an insult or injury it will be argued, "If someone broke into your house to kill you and your family, would you not defend yourself?" Extreme scenarios that few of us will ever face are thus used to discourage acts of selfless love that entail more marginal risks. Nevertheless, these very acts of selfless love can distinguish Christians. All this is to say, the selfless use and restraint of power entails risk to the power holder and those under his authority but nevertheless provides an evangelistic witness to society that fulfills the Great Commandment.

Another characteristic that should distinguish the church is unity. As members of the church, our identity should be rooted in Christ rather than anything else. "Above all, you must live as citizens of heaven, conducting yourselves in a manner worthy of the Good News about Christ."[45] Politics is greatly influenced by the collective identities we adopt, and political conflicts generally fall along the lines of income, race, geography, nationality, political affiliation, gender, etc. Yet the Bible repeatedly makes it clear that there are to be no divisions between believers. The model for Christian unity is the Trinity.[46] Paul called for Christians to be united in his instructions to the church:

> I appeal to you, dear brothers and sisters, by the authority of our Lord Jesus Christ, to live in harmony with each other. Let there be no divisions in the church. Rather, be of one mind, united in thought and purpose.[47]

45. See Philippians 1:27.
46. See John 17:20–21.
47. See 1 Corinthians 1:10.

Elsewhere Paul stated, "There is no longer Jew or Gentile, slave or free, male and female. For you are all one in Christ Jesus."[48] James likewise sharply condemned favoritism in the church that elevated some believers over others based on such distinctions.[49] A Christian perspective on politics should therefore not be based on the ephemeral, superficial, distinctions that drive worldly politics. Christians should see each other as brothers and sisters in Christ no matter their race, nationality, politics, etc. and seek not only their own interests but also the interests of others. "Don't look out only for your own interests, but take an interest in others, too."[50] Other Christians should be the first (yet not the last) recipient of selfless love from Christians.

Rooting our identity in nothing but Christ also means that our identity should not be rooted in what we might call our "image" or what others think about us. In politics, a favorable public image translates into political power. For this reason, those desiring authority spend great effort cultivating their image—history is littered with examples of political leaders going so far as to present themselves as a god to the people they govern.[51] And yet the Bible teaches through commands and examples that Christians should have little regard for their image.

Jesus himself expresses little concern when others think him insane, demonic, or misunderstand him to be just another prophet.[52] In the Old Testament, we see David joyfully dancing "with all his might" before the Lord as the Ark of the Covenant is being carried into Jerusalem. David's wife Michael criticizes him for

48. See Galatians 3:28.

49. James even questions the salvation of those who do so. See James 2:1–4.

50. See Philippians 2:4.

51. For an example in the Bible, see Darius the Mede's edict that people should only pray to him in Daniel 6.

Notably, the Mayo Clinic describes "a deep need for excessive attention and admiration" as a symptom of narcissism.

52. See John 10:20 or Mark 3:21 for examples. Notably in Matthew 16:13–20, when the apostles tell Jesus that the public widely believes him to be a prophet, Jesus "sternly warns" them not to reveal his true identity as the Messiah.

"shamelessly exposing himself to the servant girls like any vulgar person might do!" And yet David replies, "I am willing to look even more foolish than this, even to be humiliated in my own eyes!"[53] God praises other Old Testament kings, including both the godly and the wicked, for their humility when they set aside the trappings of power and seek forgiveness through prayer, fasting, and the wearing of sackcloth.[54] Paul provides another excellent example of the Christian disregard of image.

Paul expresses little concern when the Roman governor Festus considers him insane for preaching the gospel.[55] When the Corinthian church is quarreling over whether Paul or Apollos is the best leader, Paul instructs them to see both Apollos and himself as "mere servants" of Christ, adding, "it matters very little how I might be evaluated by you or by any human authority. I don't even trust my own judgment on this point."[56] Later in 2 Corinthians, Paul says, "If it seems we are crazy, it is to bring glory to God."[57] Paul had much to boast about—he could have easily cultivated the image of a "super-apostle" but he said, "I won't do it, because I don't want anyone to give me credit beyond what they can see in my life or hear in my message."[58]

Politically, a disregard of image liberates Christians from the burdensome task of cultivating an image before society. Christians, whether privately or publically expressing their views, need not be concerned about how society responds. Society may regard the Christian's views as antiquated, narrow-minded, or even bigoted, but the Christian should only be concerned with how God regards their views. This is not to say Christians should

53. See 2 Samuel 6:20–22.

54. See 1 Kings 21:28–29 where God delays punishing Ahab and his family because Ahab humbled himself before God. Also in Jonah 3, God forgoes destroying Nineveh because the king and his people humbled themselves. Other examples include: 2 Chronicles 12:12, 32:26, 33:12, and 34:27

55. See Acts 26:24.

56. See 1 Corinthians 4:1–3.

57. See 2 Corinthians 5:13.

58. See 2 Corinthians 12:6. See 2 Corinthians 11 and 12 for Paul's impressive resume.

express their views combatively or callously. The fruit of the Spirit, that is love, gentleness, kindness, etc., should mark all actions of Christians.

Sharing a common identity in Christ is one way the church should distinguish itself from the world by its unity. How Christians resolve conflict is another way our unity should be apparent. When there is conflict between believers (as inevitably there will be), Paul presents a radical model for resolution that evangelistically sets Christians apart from the world. Rather than quarreling, Christians are to either submit conflicts to the church for arbitration or simply allow themselves to be wronged and trust that God will act in their defense. The Bible similarly calls Christians to engage in conflict (with both Christians and non-Christians) "gently."[59] On numerous occasions when Paul is in conflict with other Christians, he condemns their actions but when they fail to acknowledge the sinfulness of their ways, he simply separates from them (and instructs other Christians to do likewise) and leaves them at the hands of Satan.[60] Christians who have been wronged can trust that God will not overlook such offenses because God is passionate about justice.[61]

JUSTICE

A final key principle for a Christian perspective on politics is justice. The Bible has a lot to say about justice. In short, "the LORD loves justice."[62] The strong, at times graphic, language God uses to describe injustice testifies to his passion for justice. For example in the book of Micah, God sharply condemns Israel's wealthy for exploiting the poor and likens it to cannibalism:

59. See Titus 3:1–2, 1 Peter 3:16 and Ephesians 4:2

60. See 1 Corinthians 5:1–5 where a believer refuses to cease sexual relations with his stepmother. Paul instructs the church to simply expel the man from the church and "hand him over to Satan." Likewise in 1 Timothy 1:20, Paul "hands over to Stan" two believers who refused correction.

61. See 1 Corinthians 6:1–11.

62. See Psalm 37:28. See also Psalm 11:7 and Isaiah 61:8.

I said, "Listen, you leaders of Israel!
You are supposed to know right from wrong,
but you are the very ones
who hate good and love evil.
You skin my people alive
and tear the flesh from their bones.
Yes, you eat my people's flesh,
strip off their skin,
and break their bones.
You chop them up
like meat for the cooking pot.
Then you beg the Lord for help in times of trouble!
Do you really expect him to answer?
After all the evil you have done,
he won't even look at you!"[63]

God's passion for justice is particularly strong when the most vulnerable in society are exploited—the poor, orphans, foreigners, and widows.[64] God singles out these groups repeatedly in the Bible and explicitly declares, "Cursed is anyone who denies justice to foreigners, orphans, or widows," and the ancient Israelites were required to give a tenth of their harvest every three years to feed the poor, the widows, the orphans, and foreigners.[65]

Christians are called to use authority justly, no matter what level of authority they possess. Judges and officials are told, "They must judge the people fairly. You must never twist justice or show partiality."[66] The Israelite kings are told to "Give justice each morning to the people you judge! Help those who have been robbed; rescue them from their oppressors."[67] Notably, when Solomon asks for

63. See Micah 3:1–4.

64. See Isaiah 10:2, Zachariah 7:10, Deuteronomy 24:17–22, Psalm 94:1–7, Isaiah 1:23, etc.

65. See Deuteronomy 27:19, 14:28–29 and 26:12.

66. See Deuteronomy 16:18–19.

67. See Jeremiah 21:12.

wisdom so he can rule justly, God is "pleased" and not only gives him wisdom but also riches and fame.[68]

Justly exercising authority can be an evangelistic expression of selfless love when those in authority have nothing to gain by acting justly.[69] The poor, widows, orphans, and foreigners are not usually able to repay those in authority. The rich and powerful, on the other hand, are usually in a position to exact vengeance on authorities that prevent them from exploiting others. The vulnerable may not even appreciate the justice they receive or the self-sacrifice of the one in authority. Nevertheless, Christians in authority are called to consider the interests of others and use their authority justly because doing so is an evangelistic witness that fulfills the Great Commission.

Conversely, God sharply condemns those who use authority unjustly and promises to punish them. There are numerous examples in the Bible. One of the most direct is found in the book of Isaiah:

> What sorrow awaits the unjust judges
> 	and those who issue unfair laws.
> They deprive the poor of justice
> 	and deny the rights of the needy among my people.
> They prey on widows
> 	and take advantage of orphans.
> What will you do when I punish you,
> 	when I send disaster upon you from a distant land?
> To whom will you turn for help?
> 	Where will your treasures be safe?
> You will stumble along as prisoners
> 	or lie among the dead.
> But even then the Lord's anger will not be satisfied.
> 	His fist is still poised to strike.[70]

68. See 1 Kings 3:5–14.

69. Justly exercising authority is not always a selfless act. It can simply be a calculated maneuver to gain notoriety, wealth, or more power.

70. See Isaiah 10:1–4. For other examples see Jeremiah 5:26–31 or Jeremiah 21:12.

It is not only those in authority who are to pursue justice. All Christians are called to challenge injustice. Isaiah exhorts people to "Learn to do good. Seek justice. Help the oppressed. Defend the cause of orphans. Fight for the rights of widows."[71] Proverbs likewise calls the Godly to "Speak up for those who cannot speak for themselves; ensure justice for those being crushed. Yes, speak up for the poor and helpless, and see that they get justice."[72] The account of Esther provides a good example of challenging injustice. Esther, the Jewish queen of the Persian King Xerxes, learns of a plot by an anti-Semitic government official to massacre Jews. She boldly risks her own life to challenge the unjust plot before the king and successfully thwarts it.[73] Challenging injustice fulfills the Great Commission by providing an evangelistic witness to society that testifies to God's love for justice.

Although God calls Christians to challenge injustice and wield authority justly, he himself repeatedly promises to defend the exploited.[74] The book of Isaiah makes it clear God even intervenes when none of his followers challenge injustice:

71. See Isaiah 1:17.

72. See Proverbs 31:8–9.

73. See Esther 5 and 7.

74. There are numerous promises of justice from God in the Bible:

"He ensures that orphans and widows receive justice." (Deuteronomy 10:18)

"The Lord will give justice to his people." (Deuteronomy 32:36 and Psalms 135:14)

"God says, 'At the time I have planned, I will bring justice against the wicked.'" (Psalm 75:2)

"He gives justice to the oppressed
    and food to the hungry.
The Lord frees the prisoners.
    The Lord opens the eyes of the blind.
The Lord lifts up those who are weighed down.
    The Lord loves the godly.
The Lord protects the foreigners among us.
    He cares for the orphans and widows,
    but he frustrates the plans of the wicked." (Psalms 146:7–9)

"Many seek the ruler's favor, but justice comes from the Lord." (Proverbs 29:26)

"He will give justice to the poor and make fair decisions for the exploited." (Isaiah 11:4)

The Lord looked and was displeased
to find there was no justice.
He was amazed to see that no one intervened
to help the oppressed.
So he himself stepped in to save them with his strong arm,
and his justice sustained him.[75]

Elsewhere in Isaiah God similarly declares, "I was amazed to see that no one intervened to help the oppressed. So I myself stepped in to save them with my strong arm, and my wrath sustained me."[76] In the New Testament, Jesus taught his followers to trust God as the provider of justice through the parable of the persistent widow. In this parable, Jesus tells of a poor woman seeking justice from a godless, corrupt judge. The judge finally relents simply because he is weary of her requests. Jesus concludes, "Learn a lesson from this unjust judge. Even he rendered a just decision in the end. So don't you think God will surely give justice to his chosen people who cry out to him day and night? Will he keep putting them off? I tell you, he will grant justice to them quickly!"[77]

The account of Esther also makes it clear, God is the ultimate guarantor of justice. God saves the Jewish people through Esther's

---

"Look at my servant, whom I strengthen.
He is my chosen one, who pleases me.
I have put my Spirit upon him.
He will bring justice to the nations.
He will not shout
or raise his voice in public.
He will not crush the weakest reed
or put out a flickering candle.
He will bring justice to all who have been wronged.
He will not falter or lose heart
until justice prevails throughout the earth.
Even distant lands beyond the sea will wait for his instruction." (Isaiah 42:1–4)

"God blesses those who hunger and thirst for justice, for they will be satisfied." (Matthew 5:6)

75. See Isaiah 59:15–16.

76. See Isaiah 63:5.

77. See Luke 18:6–8.

actions, but had she failed to act, God would have saved them by another means as her uncle tells her prior to her intervention:

> Don't think for a moment that because you're in the palace you will escape when all other Jews are killed. If you keep quiet at a time like this, deliverance and relief for the Jews will arise from some other place, but you and your relatives will die. Who knows if perhaps you were made queen for just such a time as this?[78]

God's promise of justice is fulfilled repeatedly in the Bible—typically in a gradual yet severe fashion. After the Egyptians inflict injustices on the Israelites, God inflicts a series of calamitous plagues on them in a disaster so great it foreshadows the apocalypse. In another example, Ahab, the wicked and idolatrous king of Israel, wants to buy a vineyard that is owned by his neighbor Naboth. Naboth refuses to sell, and so Ahab and his wife Jezebel conspire to have him falsely accused and murdered. God again reacts gradually but severely. Ahab is eventually killed in battle after which his wife and entire family are killed following a *coup de tat*. In a picture of gruesome poetic justice, dogs devour Jezebel's dead body in the very place where Naboth died.[79]

David, even though God deemed him "a man after my own heart," is also held accountable when he has an adulterous affair with Bathsheba, the wife of his official Uriah.[80] God again reacts gradually but severely. He waits at least the better part of a year before he confronts David through the prophet Nathan but, over time, God inflicts a series of calamitous events on David as punishment. David's newly born child dies, his older son Absalom rebels against him and publically rapes his wives, Absalom is killed by David's Machiavellian general Joab, and these are just the start of David's troubles. God decreed, "From this time on, your family will live by the sword because you have despised me by taking Uriah's wife to be your own."[81]

78. See Esther 4:13–14.

79. See 2 Kings 9:34–37.

80. See Acts 13:22.

81. See 2 Samuel 12:10. For the complete story, see 2 Samuel 11–20.

Centuries later, we find wealthy Jews are outwardly going through the motions of worshiping God while exploiting the poor.[82] God once again reacts gradually but severely. The wealthy elites that once exploited the poor are themselves impoverished to the point of cannibalism during a lengthy siege. "The people who once ate the richest foods now beg in the streets for anything they can get. Those who once wore the finest clothes now search the garbage dumps for food."[83] Most either starve, are killed, or taken as slaves to a foreign country.[84] God hates injustice regardless of who is exploiting whom. God's anger burns against both Jews and gentiles when they exploit others as well as both the godly and the ungodly. Nobody is exempted.

God calls Christians to wield authority justly and to challenge injustices but also acknowledges that injustice will indefinitely be present in a fallen world:

> Don't be surprised if you see a poor person being oppressed by the powerful and if justice is being miscarried throughout the land. For every official is under orders from higher up, and matters of justice get lost in red tape and bureaucracy. Even the king milks the land for his own profit![85]

This is because God is "slow to anger," and as seen, often responds gradually to injustice, presumably to give the unjust an opportunity to acknowledge their sins and repent.[86] A fallen world will always have injustice, but God uses injustice to glorify himself by calling Christians to challenge it evangelistically and showing the world how he personally responds to it.

82. See Isaiah 1:2–20.

83. See Lamentations 4:5.

84. See Ezekiel 5.

85. See Ecclesiastes 5:8–9.

86. See Exodus 34:6 and Number 14:18.

Part 2

Obligations and their Limits

THE UNIVERSALITY OF GOD'S COMMANDS

In addition to general principles, Scripture presents a limited number of direct commands—obligations Christians have to the states they live under. Before discussing these, however, we must first say a few words about Biblical commandments. Above all else, Christians are called to obey God, yet God's commands vary by person, place, and time. Attempting to universalize God's commandments is fraught with challenges. To give a straightforward (if not absurd) example, God commanded Jonah to go to Nineveh (near present-day Mosul, Iraq) and preach a message of repentance. When Jonah refused, God had him swallowed by a great fish to change his heart and bring him into obedience. The command was obviously not a universal one. Not all Christians are obligated to go to Mosul and preach the gospel or else face wrath by aquatic megafauna. The command applied strictly to one person, at one place, at one time.

A more serious conundrum is seen with God's command to the ancient Israelites that children not be put to death for the sins of their parents.[1] Shortly thereafter, God commands these same

1. See Deuteronomy 24:16.

Israelites to kill all those living in the Promised Land including the children.[2] The ancient Israelites are also told to destroy entire Jewish cities that tolerate the worship of other gods.[3] God's command to wipe out the Canaanites and idolatrous Jewish cities superseded the command against punishing children for the sins of their parents. Other passages raise similar issues.

The same God that detests child sacrifice, praises Abraham for his willingness to sacrifice his child to God. The same God that commands Christians to love their enemies and turn the other cheek, instructs the ancient Israelites to wage war against their enemies. In Deuteronomy 23, God commands, "If slaves should escape from their masters and take refuge with you, you must not hand them over to their masters." and yet Paul sends the slave Onesimus back to his owner Philemon.[4] In short, we must concede that God's commands are not always universally applicable to all people, in all places, at all times, and therefore, a command given in once instance may contradict a command given in another instance.

This uncomfortably opens the door to moral relativism—each person deciding what God has "called" him to do no matter what Scripture says. To this, I can offer only two antidotes. Firstly, our attitude is a better indicator of obedience than our actions. The actions resulting from obedience will vary by person, place, and time, but the attitude of obedience will always be the same—one of a love for God, a love for neighbors, and actions that are marked by the fruit of the spirit. Many words and deeds can result from such an attitude.

Secondly, while God's commands *can* vary from person to place to time, they *usually* apply more broadly. God gave many commandments to the ancient Israelites, and there is no indication that specific individuals were exempted from these commands. God similarly gave the church broad commands, and there is no indication that specific individuals are exempted. Setting aside

2. See Deuteronomy 20:16–17.

3. See Deuteronomy 13:15.

4. See Deuteronomy 23:15 and Philemon 1:12.

questions of universality, the Bible offers some concrete guidance on the relationship between Christians and the state.

CHRISTIAN OBLIGATIONS

For one, Christians are generally commanded to submit to governing authorities. Romans 13 explicitly states, "Everyone must submit to governing authorities. For all authority comes from God, and those in positions of authority have been placed there by God. So anyone who rebels against authority is rebelling against what God has instituted, and they will be punished."[5] Similarly, 1 Peter 2 states, "For the Lord's sake, submit to all human authority—whether the king as head of state or the officials he has appointed. For the king has sent them to punish those who do wrong and to honor those who do right."[6] Titus 3 states, "Remind the believers to submit to the government and its officers. They should be obedient, always ready to do what is good."[7]

Christians do not submit to government authorities because the authorities are just—to the contrary, all authorities, as sinners, are unjust to some extent. Likewise, submission to fallible authorities entails a measure of risk by making us vulnerable to their rule. Christians should submit to political authorities, nevertheless, as an evangelistic act that places trust in an infallible God rather than a fallible human. As Peter goes on to note, Christians submit to authorities because "It is God's will that your honorable lives should silence those ignorant people who make foolish accusations against you."[8]

Submission entails paying taxes. Romans 13 explicitly commands Christians to pay taxes to the state because the state serves God's purposes. "Pay your taxes. . . For government workers need to be paid. They are serving God in what they do."[9] Adding

5. See Romans 13:1–2.

6. See 1 Peter 2:13–14.

7. See Titus 3:1.

8. See 1 Peter 2:15.

9. See Romans 13:6.

emphasis to this command is a curious account in Matthew 17 where Jesus instructs Peter to pay the temple tax that financially supported the High Priest and the Sanhedrin who were local governing authorities. In the account, money for the tax is provided through a miraculous event where Peter, under instructions from Christ, catches a fish and finds the money inside. If only God provided for all our tax obligations so miraculously!

In addition to the explicit command to submit to authority, the Bible indicates through example that loving our neighbors as ourselves entails broadly seeking the welfare of society. The best example of this is the ancient Jews like Daniel who were living in captivity in a pagan society under an idolatrous government. When the Babylonians conquered the southern kingdom of Judah, they forced many of the Jewish people who survived to relocate. This meant not only the end of their political independence—a devastating episode for any people—but also expulsion from the temple and the Promised Land—an event of enormous religious significance. Everything within the Jews screamed for a quick return and a restoration of their relationship with God. The Psalms capture their sentiments:

> Beside the rivers of Babylon, we sat and wept
> as we thought of Jerusalem.
> We put away our harps,
> hanging them on the branches of poplar trees.
> For our captors demanded a song from us.
> Our tormentors insisted on a joyful hymn:
> "Sing us one of those songs of Jerusalem!"
> But how can we sing the songs of the Lord
> while in a pagan land?
> If I forget you, O Jerusalem,
> let my right hand forget how to play the harp.
> May my tongue stick to the roof of my mouth
> if I fail to remember you,
> if I don't make Jerusalem my greatest joy.[10]

10. See Psalm 137:1–6.

Despite their anguish, God did not immediately open the door for their return. To the contrary, he instructed them to settle down, establish households, and seek the welfare of the pagan society around them:

> This is what the Lord of Heaven's Armies, the God of Israel, says to all the captives he has exiled to Babylon from Jerusalem: "Build homes, and plan to stay. Plant gardens, and eat the food they produce. Marry and have children. Then find spouses for them so that you may have many grandchildren. Multiply! Do not dwindle away! And work for the peace and prosperity of the city where I sent you into exile. Pray to the Lord for it, for its welfare will determine your welfare."[11]

Daniel and others faithfully followed these instructions providing loyal, effective, service to Nebuchadnezzar and the succeeding authorities. Do not miss the significance of this act. Nebuchadnezzar had militarily defeated Judah, plundered the temple, and relocated a large portion of the Jewish population. Moreover, he was forcing young men like Daniel to serve in the Babylonian government. Daniel had every reason to hate the Babylonians and seek their destruction.[12] Nevertheless, he forgave, trusted God, and provided exemplary service with a sincere attitude that was an evangelistic witness to the pagan society around him.[13]

11. See Jeremiah 29:4–7.

12. Psalm 137:7–9 illustrates the attitude of most Jews towards their Babylonian captors.

O Lord, remember what the Edomites did
    on the day the armies of Babylon captured Jerusalem.
"Destroy it!" they yelled.
    "Level it to the ground!"
O Babylon, you will be destroyed.
    Happy is the one who pays you back
    for what you have done to us.
Happy is the one who takes your babies
    and smashes them against the rocks!

13. Even Daniel's envious, bureaucratic enemies recognized his loyalty, competence, and faith in God. See Daniel 6:4–5.

This example has many modern parallels. Because of sin, Christians today, like the ancient Jews, find themselves living in a society that at best tolerates them and at worst persecutes them. Christians today, like the ancient Jews, should serve as a witness in society. Yet inwardly, everything within the Christian screams for a return to the garden of Eden and a restoration of their full relationship with God. One day for the Christian, as for the ancient Jew, there will be a restoration yet until that day the Bible indicates we should love our neighbors as ourselves and seek the welfare of the societies we live in.

In the New Testament, there are more explicit commands for Christians to support the state. At the most basic level, Christians are called to "respect the king" and give "respect and honor to those who are in authority."[14] In the same way that Daniel showed respect to pagan authorities (whatever their personal or political shortcomings), Christians are to show respect to authorities (again, whatever their personal or political shortcomings.)

Added to the obligation to respect is an obligation to intercede prayerfully for authorities. "Pray for all people. Ask God to help them; intercede on their behalf, and give thanks for them. Pray this way for kings and all who are in authority."[15] Interceding for authorities benefits the entire state, Christians included, by empowering them with Godly wisdom and strengthening them against temptations. Expressing our gratitude to God for the authorities, (a task that is admittedly difficult to do at times) checks our own attitude that can be corrupted with cynicism and hate. Most importantly, praying for authorities is an evangelistic act that Paul exhorts Christians to do, "so that we can live peaceful and quiet lives marked by godliness and dignity. This is good and pleases God our Savior, who wants everyone to be saved and to understand the truth."[16]

Finally, Christians who find themselves in positions of authority are to "take the responsibility seriously" and exercise

14. See 1 Peter 2:17 and Romans 13:7.

15. See 1 Timothy 2:1–2.

16. See 1 Timothy 2:2–4.

authority with diligence and sincerity.[17] In democratic countries, citizens have a share of authority through the right to vote, and Christians should exercise this authority seriously by praying and informing themselves on the candidates and issues.[18] Other Christians obtain positions of authority by applying for jobs with the government or running for public office. Regardless of how they obtain their authority, Christians should follow Daniel's example and exercise their authority diligently and in a manner marked by the fruit of the spirit. When they do so, they not only benefit the state and all those living under it, but they also present an evangelistic witness to society as Daniel did. At the same time, there are limits to the Christian obligations to obey and support the state. In short, Christians are not obligated to submit if submission entails sinning.

THE LIMITS OF CHRISTIAN OBLIGATIONS

There are many examples in the Bible of conflicts between the commands of the state and the commands of God. Daniel provides loyal and effective service to a number of pagan kings, and yet he openly violates a law ordering citizens to worship no one except the king under pain of death.[19] Shadrach, Meshach, and Abednego similarly provide loyal service to pagan leaders up to the point where the government orders them to bow down to an idol.[20] In the New Testament, when temple authorities arrest Peter and John for preaching the gospel, they merely reply, "Do you think God wants us to obey you rather than him?"[21]

17. See Romans 12:8.

18. While voters are often aware of the "top of ticket" candidates carrying out high profile campaigns, voters are not usually familiar with "down ballot" races—those running for state and local offices. If voters obtained a sample ballot prior to the election and spent just one hour researching the down ballot candidates and issues, it would dramatically transform the election process and arguably yield far better winners at the state and local level which would in turn yield higher quality candidates for the "top of ticket" races.

19. See Daniel 6.

20. See Daniel 3.

21. See Acts 4:19.

These cases are relatively straightforward conflicts between the commands of the state and the commands of God. Other issues are more challenging and raise questions about Christian ethics.[22] Violence is one long-debated issue. All states (by definition) hold the power of life and death and empower authorities to kill citizens under specified conditions. A police officer can shoot a criminal if they are endangering someone's life. Soldiers can kill those threatening national security.

Pacifists argue that Christians should not use violence given Christ's commands in the Sermon on the Mount:

> "You have heard the law that says the punishment must match the injury: 'An eye for an eye, and a tooth for a tooth.' But I say, do not resist an evil person! If someone slaps you on the right cheek, offer the other cheek also. If you are sued in court and your shirt is taken from you, give your coat, too. If a soldier demands that you carry his gear for a mile, carry it two miles. Give to those who ask, and don't turn away from those who want to borrow.
> "You have heard the law that says, 'Love your neighbor' and hate your enemy. But I say, love your enemies! Pray for those who persecute you! In that way, you will be acting as true children of your Father in heaven.[23]

However, these pacifistic commands do not appear to apply to those in authority. In the above passage, Christ instructs his followers to peacefully endure injustices inflicted upon them by authorities or other citizens. His examples include a civil lawsuit between citizens and an actual Roman law that permitted soldiers to force civilians to carry their gear one mile. He makes no reference

22. The concept of Christian ethics itself is problematic because, above all else, Christians are obligated to obey God, and as discussed above, God's commands are not always universally applicable to all people at all times. A code of ethics, on the other hand, is universally applicable and does not vary by person, place, and time, only by circumstance. The concept of a Christian ethic is further complicated by the fact that God occasionally commands his followers to do things that are considered unethical from earthly perspectives such as killing all the previous inhabitants of the Promised Land. (See Deuteronomy 20:16–17.)

23. See Matthew 5:38–45.

to the just use of force by someone in authority which other Biblical passages affirm. Old Testament law requires violent punishment for many crimes.[24] In the New Testament, Paul declares that authorities "are God's servants, sent for the very purpose of punishing those who do what is wrong."[25] Moreover, in Luke 3, when soldiers come to John the Baptist to be baptized, they ask him for guidance. He replies, "Don't extort money or make false accusations. And be content with your pay."[26] There is no mention of abandoning their violent service to the state. Similarly, shortly after presenting the Sermon on the Mount, Matthew records Jesus praising a Roman Centurion for his great faith—again there is no mention of Jesus calling on the Centurion to abandon his violent profession. Absence of evidence is not evidence of absence, but if Jesus' intent in the Sermon on the Mount was to declare all violence to be inherently sinful (a substantial change from Old Testament commands), then it is surprising that Jesus does not directly make the point either in the Sermon on the Mount or in his interaction with the Centurion.

While citizens are called to tolerate injustice from governments and other citizens, authorities are called to use force to prevent injustice. As noted above, God loves justice. Order is a prerequisite for justice, and maintaining any measure of either requires the use of force. For this reason, states should (and inevitably will) use violence to maintain their authority. Law enforcement officers will use violence to defend state authority from internal challenges. The military will use violence to defend state authority from external challenges. Given that Christians are generally called to submit to authority and wield authority justly, there is no contradiction in principle when Christians use violence to defend state authority from both internal and external challenges. However, there are limits. Christians must use violence (like any other form of authority) justly because using authority unjustly is inherently sinful. At a minimum, this suggests violence should not be used against those who are not challenging the state's authority. Saul's son Jonathan

24. See Genesis 9:6, for example, where God says, "If anyone takes a human life, that person's life will also be taken by human hands."

25. See Romans 13:4.

26. See Luke 3:14.

provides a model for how Christians should respond if they are asked to use their authority unjustly.

In 1 Samuel 19, we find David providing loyal, effective service to Saul, the king of Israel. Saul, however, is jealous of David and urges his servants and Jonathan to assassinate David. Jonathan refuses to carry out Saul's instructions. Instead, he warns David and boldly confronts Saul, challenging the unjust order:

> "The king must not sin against his servant David," Jonathan said. "He's never done anything to harm you. He has always helped you in any way he could. Have you forgotten about the time he risked his life to kill the Philistine giant and how the Lord brought a great victory to all Israel as a result? You were certainly happy about it then. Why should you murder an innocent man like David? There is no reason for it at all!"[27]

Saul temporarily relents. When he later tries to kill David again, Jonathan and his sister Michal, David's wife, once more defy Saul's authority and refuse to cooperate with his unjust effort.[28]

Externally, the principle of only using violence against those challenging state authority means violence should not be used against a foreign state (or non-state actors) unless that state is challenging the authority of another state.[29] In other words, a Christian authority is free to use military force to defend his own or his allies' authority, but he should not use it to challenge the authority of a foreign state simply because that state is seeking its own interests or committing internal injustices. The Christian authority respects external authority by recognizing the sovereignty of foreign states and acknowledging that all states are unjust to some degree.

Lying presents another issue of Christian ethics and a point of tension between the commands of the state and the commands of God. Scripture condemns lying and refers to Satan as the "father of lies." The Ten Commandments prohibits "false testimony." Proverbs

27. See 1 Samuel 19:4–5.

28. See 1 Samuel 19–20.

29. God's command for the ancient Israelites to conquer the Promised Land would be an obvious exception to this general principle.

says God hates and detests "a lying tongue."[30] At the same time, state officials sometimes lie in the course of their duties. Law enforcement and intelligence officers lie when they go undercover. Government representatives (including Presidents and other elected officials) frequently lie for the sake of national security.[31] This raises the question of whether Christians working for the government sin if they lie in the course of their duties.

The example of Rahab the prostitute presents an interesting Biblical case for consideration.[32] In Joshua 2, Joshua secretly sends Israelite spies to Jericho on the eve of their siege. The spies spend the night in the home of a prostitute named Rahab, but they are spotted. The king of Jericho orders Rahab to bring out the spies. Rabab, however, lies and says they have already left her home.[33] The books of Hebrews and James later praise her for her faithful actions.[34] God also places Rahab in the genealogical line of Jesus.[35] Notably, however, Scripture does not specifically praise her for the lie but rather for hiding them and sending them away safely.

Curiously, the sending of spies in itself may have indicated a lack of faith. In Deuteronomy, Moses recounts how the sending of scouts ultimately led to sin when the Israelites first came to the Promised Land:

> I said to you, 'You have now reached the hill country of the Amorites that the Lord our God is giving us. Look! He has placed the land in front of you. Go and occupy

30. See Proverbs 6:17

31. A typical example is when members of the press ask about clandestine troop deployments. To acknowledge their deployment would put their lives at risk.

32. 1 Samuel 16 presents another case for consideration. The prophet Samuel is told to go to Bethlehem and anoint David king of Israel, but Samuel fears King Saul will kill him if he does so. God essentially instructs Samuel to use the "cover story" of going to Bethlehem to offer a sacrifice to God. Samuel does not lie (he actually offers the sacrifice) but apparently deceives Saul all the same.

33. See Joshua 2.

34. See Hebrews 11:31 and James 2:25.

35. See Matthew 1:5.

> it as the Lord, the God of your ancestors, has promised you. Don't be afraid! Don't be discouraged!'
>
> "But you all came to me and said, 'First, let's send out scouts to explore the land for us. They will advise us on the best route to take and which towns we should enter.'
>
> "This seemed like a good idea to me, so I chose twelve scouts, one from each of your tribes. They headed for the hill country and came to the valley of Eshcol and explored it. They picked some of its fruit and brought it back to us. And they reported, 'The land the Lord our God has given us is indeed a good land.'
>
> "But you rebelled against the command of the Lord your God and refused to go in."[36]

Moses may be hinting that the people wanted to use scouts because they were afraid. Arguably, there was no reason to send out scouts. God had already allotted the land to them and guaranteed victory no matter which route was taken or which towns were entered.

No matter what Moses may be suggesting here, the case of Rahab appears at most to be an exception to a general prohibition against lying. Christians in authority should not lie in an effort to maintain state authority. Undercover and clandestine operations may marginally help maintain state authority, but the use of sinful actions to maintain authority indicates that the Christian is ultimately putting their trust in such measures rather than God.

Another hotly debated issue is submission to unjust laws. As noted above, God is passionate about justice and calls on Christians to challenge injustices. This raises the question of whether Christians are obligated to obey an unjust law. First, we must reset our expectations. Because those in authority are but mere sinners (like everyone else) all states will be unjust to some degree—perfect government is not attainable this side of Paradise. Christians should expect a measure of injustice. Secondly, we must distinguish between laws that demand sinful behavior and laws that are merely unjust.

36. See Deuteronomy 1:20–26.

The ancient Muslim practice of *jizya* presents an example of a law that was unjust but did not require Christians to sin. The *jizya* was a special tax Islamic governments placed on non-Muslims during the Middle Ages. We may bristle at the thought of such discrimination, but complying with the law required no sin on the Christian's part. God does not prohibit paying taxes, to the contrary he commands it. Christians are thus obligated to pay taxes—even if they are discriminatory and unjust. It is not a sin to suffer injustice—Christ proved that by dying on the cross.

Another admittedly controversial example is southern segregation laws that discriminated against African Americans. Black Christians suffered injustices under these laws, like Christians in our earlier example of *jizya* taxes, but the law did not require them to sin, only to suffer an injustice.[37] Paul provides a model of how to respond. When Paul encounters racial segregation, on the part of Peter no less, he sharply condemns it, but there is no indication that he attempts to force Peter into following God's commands.[38] Peter was eventually convicted of his sin and voluntarily reformed. Paul also provides a model when condemnation fails to bring repentance (as it did in the case of white segregationists). On numerous occasions, he simply separates from (that is to say excommunicates) Christians who stubbornly refuse to repent of their blatantly sinful ways and "hands them over to Satan."[39] As challenging as it is to

37. Notably, segregation laws did require white Christians to sin by discriminating against black Christians. God commanded Christians not to discriminate against each other (James 2:1–4) and this command supersedes any earthly law. White Christians should have therefore welcomed black Christians into their homes, businesses, and churches regardless of what the laws said. However, the obvious heart of the problem was not that non-Christians were forcing white Christians to discriminate against blacks, but rather that white Christians were blatantly disregarding God's command.

38. Paul was refusing to eat with gentile believers who, because of their race, had not been circumcised. Thankfully, it seems Paul, Barnabus, and others quickly realized the error of their ways after being rebuked by Paul. See Galatians 2:11–14.

39. See 1 Corinthians 5:1–5 where a believer refuses to cease sexual relations with his stepmother. Paul instructs the church to simply expel the man from the church and "hand him over to Satan." Likewise in 1 Timothy 1:19–20, Paul "hands over to Satan" two believers who refused correction.

acknowledge, the Bible provides no support that Christians are free to disobey unjust laws simply because they are unjust. God is the ultimate guarantor of justice and will deal with the unjust in his own way, in his own time.

Similarly, Christians are not free to disobey just laws for the sake of protesting an unjust law. For example, laws prohibiting trespassing, the defacement of property, and the destruction of property are necessary for maintaining order and ownership of property. There is nothing inherently unjust about them. Nevertheless, protestors occasionally break these laws by hanging banners, painting signs, holding sit-ins, etc. without the consent of the property owners. We can be sympathetic to these tactics when they halt injustices. Yet from a Christian perspective, we should not judge the actions by the outcomes (which are beyond our control) but rather by Scripture and God's commands. The Roman and Babylonian governments no doubt had many unjust laws, and yet there is no record of Paul or Daniel violating just laws to protest against unjust laws.[40]

When Christians must disobey laws because submission entails sinning, it is helpful to distinguish between civil disobedience and rebellion. Civil disobedience is when someone knowingly disobeys the law and willingly suffers the legal consequences of their actions. When Paul is arrested, he follows the example of Jesus and goes willingly without resistance.[41] When Shadrach, Meshach, and Abednego are arrested and brought before King Nebuchadnezzar, they simply say, "O Nebuchadnezzar, we do not need to defend ourselves before you."[42]

40. This is not to say that Christians should not use their political rights to call attention to injustices legally. (See discussion below on the exercise of legal rights.) Multiple scriptures command Christians to speak out against injustice. For example, Isaiah 1:17 says, "Learn to do good. Seek justice. Help the oppressed. Defend the cause of orphans. Fight for the rights of widows." Likewise, Proverbs 31:8–9 says, "Speak up for those who cannot speak for themselves; ensure justice for those being crushed. Yes, speak up for the poor and helpless, and see that they get justice." (See the discussion of justice in Part 1 for more on this.)

41. See Acts 21:33.

42. See Daniel 3:16.

Rebellion, on the other hand, is when someone disobeys with the intent of overthrowing the existing government, usually through violent means. As previously mentioned in Romans 13, 1 Peter 2, and Titus 3, Christians are generally commanded to submit to governing authorities and, to my knowledge, there is only one example in the Bible of God calling a specific individual to rebel against their government. In 2 Kings 9, God instructs Jehu to revolt against Joram king of Israel, son of Ahab. "I anoint you king over the Lord's people Israel. *You are to destroy the house of Ahab your master.*"[43] Jehu then carries out a bloody *coup de tat* against Joram, killing him, his mother, his friends, his officials, and his entire family as well as the king of Judah (who was a relative of Joram). Finally, Jehu concocts an elaborate scheme to kill all the prophets of Baal. He invites them to worship in Baal's temple and personally offers a sacrifice to Baal in order to deceive them. Jehu's men then kill everyone in the temple. Afterward, God praises Jehu's actions saying, "You have done well in following my instructions to destroy the family of Ahab."[44] (Notably, God does not specifically praise Jehu for lying or offering the sacrifice to Baal.) Jehu's rebellion was violent, deceitful, and bloody. And yet God instructed him to revolt and affirmed his actions afterward. His example, however, appears to be an exception to the general rule against rebellion.

The command to submit to authority does not mean that Christians cannot exercise the rights given to them by the state. Paul repeatedly made use of his political rights. In Acts 16, city officials in Philippi arrest and beat him on false charges. The next day they order him freed, but Paul insists they personally release him because it was illegal to arrest and beat him—a Roman citizen—without a trial. Alarmed, the city officials go to Paul and apologize.[45] In Acts 22, when a Roman soldier is about to whip Paul, Paul uses his rights as a Roman citizen to challenge the legality of the act. The commander immediately halts the proceedings.[46] In Acts 25, Paul

43. Italics added. See 2 Kings 9:7.

44. See 2 Kings 10:30.

45. See Acts 16:16–40.

46. See Acts 22:24–29.

is under arrest in Caesarea and Jewish officials are requesting his transfer to Jerusalem so they can kill him *en route*. Wise to their schemes, Paul insists on a trial in a Roman court and appeals to Caesar.[47] These examples show that Christians are free to exercise their rights when they choose to.

When Christians exercise their political rights, they must do so in a Godly manner. The fruit of the spirit should mark Christian behavior in political circumstances like any other circumstance. Christians can boldly exercise their rights, but they should do so lovingly and respectfully and with the knowledge that evangelism rather that political change is the ultimate goal. When Christians inevitably fall short of this standard, they should acknowledge it and apologize. Paul again provides a model when the high priest orders Paul slapped in the mouth:

> Instantly Ananias the high priest commanded those close to Paul to slap him on the mouth. But Paul said to him, "God will slap you, you corrupt hypocrite! What kind of judge are you to break the law yourself by ordering me struck like that?"
>
> Those standing near Paul said to him, "Do you dare to insult God's high priest?"
>
> "I'm sorry, brothers. I didn't realize he was the high priest," Paul replied, "for the Scriptures say, 'You must not speak evil of any of your rulers.'"[48]

Christians also need to have a Biblical rather than a contemporary perspective of political rights. It is helpful to distinguish the two. Contemporary political culture readily speaks of human rights. The concept has long roots in Western political thought and is widely (if sometimes lightly) used today in political discourse. Yet the original meaning is important to understand. The English philosopher John Locke offered one of the most influential definitions of "rights." In his view, God had granted to man certain unalienable rights the most important of which was the right to life and property. Since he saw these rights coming from God, he felt

47. See Acts 25:1–12.

48. See Acts 23:2–5. The scripture Paul quotes is Exodus 22:28.

no government could take away your life or property without your consent. People therefore collectively chose which form of government they lived under, how much authority the government had, and when the government could take away their property or life. If the government attempted to take away people's property or life without their consent, then the people had not only the option *but also the obligation to* overthrow the government using force if necessary.[49] These ideas form the philosophical foundation of democratic government and are so ingrained in contemporary culture that we rarely question them. And yet we see no such system of rights and obligations in the Bible.

Paul, when counseling persecuted Christians in the Roman Empire, urges submission rather than revolution. Likewise, when Shadrach, Meshach, and Abednego are arrested and given a death sentence for refusing to worship an idol, they make no appeal to a God-given right to life. They do not call for a revolution. They simply refuse to submit to a law that requires them to sin and accept the legal punishment.[50] Daniel reacts in a similar way when he is sentenced to death for praying to God.[51] As difficult as it is for our contemporary culture to accept, Christians are not free to rebel against authority simply because the government is not sufficiently protecting our life or property or granting us the freedoms that we are so accustomed to today. On the contrary, the Bible tells us to expect earthly governments to act unjustly. In 1 Samuel, God warns the people about earthly rulers:

> So Samuel passed on the Lord's warning to the people who were asking him for a king. "This is how a king will reign over you," Samuel said. "The king will draft your sons and assign them to his chariots and his charioteers, making them run before his chariots. Some will be generals and captains in his army, some will be forced to plow in his fields and harvest his crops, and some will make his weapons and chariot equipment. The king will take your daughters from you and force them to cook

49. See John Locke's "Second Treatise on Government."

50. See Daniel 3.

51. See Daniel 6.

> and bake and make perfumes for him. He will take away the best of your fields and vineyards and olive groves and give them to his own officials. He will take a tenth of your grain and your grape harvest and distribute it among his officers and attendants. He will take your male and female slaves and demand the finest of your cattle and donkeys for his own use. He will demand a tenth of your flocks, and you will be his slaves. When that day comes, you will beg for relief from this king you are demanding, but then the Lord will not help you."[52]

Theologically speaking, it is foolish to expect justice from a government all the time. Governing authorities are but mere sinners who, in their fallen state, will inevitably sin just like anyone else. Power in the hands of sinners will be used unjustly. Again, it is difficult to accept this from our modern vantage point where we are taught that governments are obligated to provide for the people and if they do not, the people are obligated to overthrow it. Unfortunately, such expectations run counter to not only human history but also Biblical descriptions of the fallen state of humanity. All this is to say that Christians, like Paul, can freely exercise the rights granted to them by their governments, but they should not be deceived into believing that the government owes them certain rights, freedoms, or material things such as healthcare and education. If governments provide such things, Christians should be grateful. If they do not, Christians have no Biblical basis for using force to obtain them.

52. See 1 Samuel 8:10–18.

Part 3

Practice

Having outlined the broad principles for a Christian perspective of government and politics as well as the more explicit guidance Scripture gives on obligations and their limits, let us now paint a picture of how Christians should interact with their governments.

THE CHRISTIAN CITIZEN

In general, the Christian citizen is supportive of the state and submissive to its authority. They live a "quiet life," obeying the laws, paying taxes, completing whatever work is before them, "as though you were working for the Lord rather than for people," and loving their neighbors while they love God.[1] In other words, they are productive members of society who help those in need. The Christian citizen prays for authorities and expresses both gratitude and respect for their service. At the same time, they recognize that even the best of leaders, those who they most agree with politically, are but fallen sinners inclined to do evil. For this reason, the Christian citizen does not put their hope in a political leader or movement; they place it solely and firmly in Jesus Christ knowing that Christ is their sovereign and just provider of all things.

1. See 1 Thessalonians 4:11 and Colossians 3:23.

The Christian citizen grieves the sin in society, prays for that society, and confesses the sins of the church, both individually and corporately. They do this as a sincere expression of grief, as an act of faith that God will alleviate the damage caused by sin, and as a way of communicating to the world God's standard of morality. All three provide an evangelistic witness to society. At the same time, they do not judge non-Christians or society as a whole. They are not "disappointed" in the sinfulness of non-Christians because they have no expectation that non-Christians will behave or think like Christians.

The Christian citizen is free to engage in political discourse or exercise their state-given rights, but they do so in a gentle, respectful, loving manner. They have little concern for how society judges their political motives or values because their identity is rooted in Christ. In democratic countries, the Christian citizen thoughtfully and prayerfully votes as a way of diligently exercising the authority God has entrusted to them. When advocating for political issues or voting, the Christian citizen considers not just their own interests but also the interests of other people, both foreign and domestic. The Christian citizen supports restraint on the accumulation and use of power, no matter who is using or accumulating the power because they know even the best leaders will fall prey to the temptations that come with great power. Moreover, they understand that broadly considering the interests of all and restraining the use of power entails a measure of risk, but they do it anyway because evangelism, rather than political change is their ultimate goal. They see God, not the government, as their ultimate and faithful provider. They see prayer, not political activism, as the true path to political change. At the same time, Christians have no illusions that non-Christians will reciprocate such acts, adhere to a Christian perspective on political issues, or be swayed by Biblical arguments. For the Christian citizen, political engagement is an act of selfless love. It is not a means to achieving an end but an end in itself.

The Christian citizen will selflessly challenge injustice in a gentle, respectful, loving, and generally legal, manner, particularly when the most vulnerable in society are being exploited. They have little concern for any social stigmas that come as a consequence of defending those whom society despises because their identity is in Christ, not race, class, societal prestige, or some other superficial distinction. At the same time, they will soberly recognize that in a fallen world, there will always be some measure of injustice. They have no illusions that respectful, legal, dissent is a guaranteed path to political change. They know prayer is more effective than political activism. They understand that challenging injustice entails a measure of risk to themselves, their families, and churches, but they do it anyway. They know God may grant success to their effort, but they also know he may not for reasons only he fully understands. Either way, Christians challenge injustice in a godly manner not because it is the most effective strategy for change, but because it is a selfless act, an evangelistic witness to society whatever the outcome.

The Christian citizen will submit to unjust laws and more broadly tolerate the injustices inflicted upon them by a world that will inevitably unwelcome their presence. They are free to use their political rights to challenge the injustices inflicted on them as they would any other injustice. And yet they will do so in a gentle, respectful, legal, manner. They know prayer is the primary path to justice. They challenge injustices not as a means of effecting political change but as a means of providing an evangelistic witness to society. They can do so because they know that God is passionate about justice and the ultimate guarantor of justice. They know that he hears their prayers and will inevitably respond even when no one else takes note of their suffering.

When Christians cannot submit to authority without sinning, they will lovingly and respectfully engage in limited, civil disobedience and suffer whatever consequences come as a result. They know God may protect them from the consequences of their actions or use their actions as a way of bringing about political change. Alternatively, he may not. Nevertheless, they do not see civil disobedience as a strategy for political change but a way of evangelistically witnessing to society. The Christian citizen can willingly defy authority whatever the outcome because they have faith that this life is "but a breath," and that "living means living for Christ, and dying is even better."[2] For this same reason, the Christian citizen does not use violence to rebel "against what God has instituted."[3]

THE CHRISTIAN AUTHORITY

Christians playing a direct role in governing, either by choice or by circumstance, have a particular obligation to know God's word and follow all the obligations of the Christian citizen because of the authority they wield[4] The Christian authority prays for those under their authority and leads the church in individually and corporately confessing the sins of society.

The Christian authority will exercise their authority justly. If laws or higher authorities demand that the Christian authority wield power unjustly, the Christian authority will refuse, as Jonathan did, and suffer whatever consequences come as a result. This includes demands to lie or use violence against those who are not challenging the state's authority. The Christian authority considers the interests of not just their own constituents but of all people—particularly the most vulnerable: widows, orphans, the poor, and foreigners. This requires the humility to recognize that others, including political opponents and outside constituents, have legitimate interests. Domestically, this means acknowledging and taking into consideration the interests of both political supporters and opponents and, importantly, seeking compromises that benefit all. Internationally, this means acknowledging and taking into consideration the interests of both domestic and foreign peoples and, importantly, forging compromises that benefit all.

The Christian authority is not naïve and does not see compromise and consensus as guarantees for popular favor. They recognize the risks associated with compromise and considering the interests of others. Political supporters, as sinners, are likely to be angered when concessions are made to political opponents.

2. See Job 7:7 and Philippians 1:21.

3. See Romans 13:2.

4. Old Testament kings, in fact, were instructed to make their own copy of the law by hand. See Deuteronomy 17:18.

Political opponents, as sinners, are unlikely to be grateful for such concessions or switch allegiances because they know someone from their own ranks will more fully cater to their interests. Nevertheless, compromising and seeking a consensus that takes into account the interests of both political supporters and opponents is a self-sacrificing act of selfless love that provides an evangelistic witness to society. It is done not as a political strategy, but because it reflects God's love into society.

When Christian authorities engage in political debate, they (like all Christians) are obligated to be gracious, gentle, and respectful to others, including political opponents—both foreign and domestic. The Christian authority will accurately characterize opposing viewpoints, acknowledge the legitimate interests of others, and peacefully petition those with greater authority. The Christian authority will pray for their political opponents. At the same time, the Christian authority can present their views boldly with little regard for how society interprets their motives or values—the Christian authority is concerned with pleasing God, not men. Bold political stands can be an act of selfless love that articulates God's standard of morality and provides an evangelistic witness to society. While the Christian authority will engage in political debate selflessly, they recognize that in a fallen world, politics will be a brutal, at times violent, sport. Grandstanding, demonizing, misleading, and lying are the native language of political debate. Violence is historically how political conflicts are ultimately resolved.

The Christian authority recognizes that restrained engagement in political debate does not guarantee political success. On the contrary, it entails risks. Brutal measures are used because they are effective. "The children of this world are more shrewd in dealing with the world around them than are the children of the light."[5] Christians engaging in political debate will be at a disadvantage to political opponents who use such tactics. And yet the Christian authority will not use these tactics because they have faith that God is sovereign and the guarantor of justice. The ultimate goal of the Christian

5. See Luke 16:8.

authority is not to bring about political change but to present an evangelistic witness to society that fulfills the Great Commission.

The Christian authority will recognize that, as a sinner, they will inevitably fall short of God's commands. At times, they will overstep their authority, wield power unjustly, engage in political debate in a mean-spirited manner, or simply be wrong in their political views. On those occasions, the Christian authority will acknowledge their shortcomings and apologize—even if it is not politically expedient. The Christian authority's identity is in Christ, not how the public perceives them. The humility of such actions will present a witness to society as much as when the authority acts justly and lovingly.

The Christian authority will restrain their accumulation and use of power, both domestically and internationally. They will restrain their accumulation of power because they know, as a mere sinner, the accumulation of vast power will present temptations the authority will inevitably fall into. At the same time, the Christian authority acknowledges the risks associated with restraining the accumulation and use of power—risks that will be borne by both the authority and those under their authority. The Christian authority has no illusions that restraining power will guarantee goodwill or reciprocal actions. They restrain the use of power, not as a strategy for political change, but because doing so provides an evangelistic witness to society that contrasts with the way the world uses power. It is an act of faith that trusts the security and wellbeing of the nation to God rather than the state.

Above all, the Christian authority remembers that the future is in God's hands, not their own. The Christian authority can restrain their use of power, take into account the interests of others, and act in a loving manner (despite the risks) because they do not rely on their own limited knowledge, wisdom, and foresight but rather on a loving, sovereign God. The success of the Christian authority is judged not by the extent of the political influence and victories but by the extent to which their engagement with government and politics provides an evangelistic witness to society that glorifies God.

CHRISTIAN POLITICS

Historically, the church has advocated for a wide range of political issues considering each in its own day to be an example of "Christian" politics. During the Reformation Era, questions of official state doctrines and worship practices dominated the debate. During the Civil War, both pro and anti-slavery Christians argued that Scripture supported their side. During the Progressive Era, tariffs, monetary policy, and labor standards were the "Christian" issues of the day. In contemporary times, the church has focused on social issues like abortion and gay marriage. Yet the Bible provides little if any direct guidance on the day-to-day matters of government policy. Values and issues vary so greatly by place and time that it is difficult if not impossible to identify policies that are universally "Christian." Some have argued that most Old Testament laws are still universally applicable today, but this seems an obvious case of universalizing commands that had more narrow application.[6] Contemporary Christians are not obligated to wear tassels on their clothing.[7] The theocratic laws presented in the Old Testament were given to a particular society at a particular time. If the law had been diligently followed, the result would have been a rough approximation of heaven-on-earth—still corrupt and sinful but nevertheless a foretaste of heaven. The law was not diligently followed, however, because sinful people do not fully submit themselves to God's will. Replicating the effort, without the unique presence and role God played in the case of the ancient Jews, would inevitably result in failure. Human nature has not changed.

More often than not, political opinions are not a matter of competing values but rather the relative balance between widely shared values. For example, most agree that liberty and security are desirable. Balancing the two, however, is difficult and very different policies can be espoused if one value is emphasized over the other. Tellingly, Jesus recruited two disciples from politically opposite extremes. The key political question in his day was the response to

6. Christian Reconstructionist theology attempts to do just this—argue that most Old Testament laws are still applicable.

7. See Numbers 15:37–39.

Roman occupation. Matthew the tax collector was a Roman collaborator. Simon the Zealot was pledged to overthrow Roman rule at all costs. (I sometimes wonder if Jesus paired the two when he sent the twelve out to preach, heal the sick, and cast out demons—what interesting conversation that would have made.) All this is to say, Christians must be humble and gracious when considering political opinions they disagree with. In general, political differences are not a matter of right and wrong but a difference of opinion and the relative importance of agreed values. There are limits, however.

At times, political views will not merely be a difference of opinion but a difference of right and wrong. Yet even when political issues are no longer a difference of opinion but a matter of right and wrong, Christians must be humble and gracious towards one another. All Christians are sinners, and sometimes our political views reflect our sinfulness. We should treat Christians who espouse sinful political opinions in the same way we would treat Christians struggling with any other sin—graciously to a large extent and then finally with excommunication.

Finally, there can be a point at which a political view is so antithetical to Christianity that it reveals the person who claims to be a Christian does not, in fact, have the Holy Spirit within them. For example, if the person were advocating for exclusive and mandatory worship of Satan, it would provide ample evidence that the person is not a Christian. Such cases are rare, however, and we must not be too quick to claim a question of opinion or sin is evidence that someone does not have the Holy Spirit living within them.

All this is to say that, Christians must be leery of considering specific policies to be "Christian" or "Non-Christian." They must humbly and graciously consider opposing viewpoints and be slow to denounce a political view as "wrong," "sinful," or "heretical." There is a point where these lines are crossed, but history shows the church has been all too quick to use these labels when it becomes engaged in politics.

CONCLUDING THOUGHTS

The church has long debated the role Christians should play in government and politics. At one extreme are those who advocate for Christian theocracies. At the other end of the spectrum are those who advocate for complete withdrawal from politics. The central question has been how to reconcile the Great Commission with the fact that politics has been and always will be an ugly, often violent, affair. Yet we must not see government and politics different from any other field Christians may find themselves engaged in. The fields of business, education, religion, and entertainment, for example, all present their own inherent challenges for Christians engaged in those fields. Yet it would be foolish to argue that Christians should not be engaged in any of those fields simply because of the temptations and challenges they present. For the church to retreat from any field in society is to yield it to Satan. The field of government and politics is no different. The question is not whether Christians should categorically disengage from this field—Christians are engaged in the field whether they recognize it or not because they live in political societies under the authority of governments. The question is how Christians, particularly those who play a substantial role, can conduct themselves in a way that fulfills the Great Commission by providing an evangelistic witness to society. This is a key question Christians face no matter what field they are in. My hope is that the thoughts and sketch provided here will help Christians navigate these challenging questions in a manner that glorifies God.

www.ingramcontent.com/pod-product-compliance
Lightning Source LLC
Chambersburg PA
CBHW051709090426
42736CB00013B/2612